Y0-AGK-850

AQUAVIT TO ZOMBIE

BASIC AND EXOTIC DRINKS

COMPILED BY PETER BEILENSON
ILLUSTRATED BY RUTH McCREA

Peter Pauper Press Mt. Vernon, N. Y.

THIS BOOK

IS DEDICATED TO

SOCIABILITY

MODERATION

EXPERIMENTATION

AND

ENJOYMENT

Aquavit or AKVAVIT (from *aqua vitae* — water of life). A colorless Scandinavian liquor, flavored with caraway. It is made by redistilling grain or potato alcohol with the flavoring ingredients. Should be served ice-cold, but not with ice—chill the bottle. Aquavit looks like gin or vodka, but its caraway flavor makes it a poor mixer. It is an excellent aperitif by itself.

Absinthe. A green liquor of anise flavor, derived from wormwood. In its original form this liquor was considered poisonous, and its manufacture was forbidden. Pernod, an equivalent substitute from the original manufacturer, is harmless, and is a common drink at Paris cafés. It is usually served with ice and water.

Amer Picon. A bitter French liquor which, diluted and sweetened, makes an aperitif.

Angostura. The commonest variety of bitters. To be used, but with moderation, in the Manhattan, Old-fashioned, Champagne and other cocktails.

Agras. An Algerian sweet soft drink: grape juice, water, sugar and crushed almonds — should be ice cold.

Aguardiente. Spanish name for firewater: raw brandy or rum.

Amers. French for Bitters.

Aperitif. An appetizer; normally an aromatic wine: Vermouth, Dubonnet, Byrrh, St. Raphael, "Martini", etc. — also dry Sherries. In Europe these are generally served at room temperature. The spices in these sweetish wines are supposed to stimulate the appetite; but American taste prefers something dry and cold as an aperitif.

Applejack. A distillation from apple mash; as opposed to true Apple Brandy, a distillation from fermented Apple Cider. Since Applejack is apt to be home-made, it is likely to be sampled young — when it is, like any young liquor, rough and tough.

Armagnac. A French brandy, similar to Cognac; but not entitled to that name since it does not come from that district.

6

Arrack. A distillation from rice, prepared in India and the Dutch East Indies. The same name is given to distillations from palm juice, molasses-and-rice, etc.

Asali. An East African fermentation from honey; similar to Mead.

Asti Spumanti. A sweet, white sparkling wine, from Italy.

Bacardi. The best-known name among rum manufacturers. The best Bacardi is made in Cuba, and the best of that is the Añejo, seldom seen in the United States. Use white label in the Bacardi cocktail.

Barsac. Wine district of the Bordeaux area; its wines are generally white.

Beaujolais. Red wine of the Burgundy area and type.

Benedictine. A sweet after-dinner liqueur, highly aromatic, made according to secret formula by the Benedictine Society in France. The letters D.O.M. on the label stand for "Deo Optimo Maximo" — "God best and greatest."

Bitters. A seasoning and blending liquor valuable in the Manhattan, Champagne, Old-fashioned and other cocktails. Angostura, the best-known, and Peychaud, used in the Sazerac cocktail, are of the aromatic type. There are also orange bitters. A simple and good cocktail can be made by adding a few dashes of bitters to gin, whisky, etc. — and stirring with ice.

Black Velvet. Half cold stout and half cold champagne, poured together, or mixed together, in a goblet or large wineglass.

Bordeaux. The name given to wines of the Bordeaux district in France, the most bountiful and famous of all wine districts. Ordinary Bordeaux bottlings are dealers' blends of various years and vineyards (plus Algerian wine in most cases); the best are chateau-bottled, each at its own vineyard, so labeled, and carrying the date of vintage. As a general rule, the best vintages are the odd years in the 1940's, and 1950, 1952, 1953, 1955.

Bourbon. American whisky made mostly from corn. It is the quickest-maturing of the three major kinds of whisky, and

therefore — if aged the same number of years — the mellowest. The "sour mash" type is the best.

Brandy. A distillation from grape wine if not otherwise described. In a broader sense, a liquor distilled from any fermented fruit. The best grape brandy comes from the Cognac district in France, and the best of Cognacs is *Fine Champagne* — which has nothing to do with bubbly Champagne, but gets its name from the Grand Champagne (big field) district in the Cognac area.

Buck. A long drink made with lemon and ginger ale and, usually, gin. Sugar or other sweetening is not used in a Buck.

Burgundy. Wine made in the small district in central France which is appropriately named (because of the value of its vineyards and their product) the Côte d'Or, or Gold Coast. Burgundies are usually red, heavy-bodied, and bland; they are served at room temperature, with red meats. There is no chateau bottling, as in Bordeaux wines; most Burgundies are dealers' blends, although wine from

10

the most famous vineyards is kept separate and specially-labeled. Vintage years are important: in general the odd years of the 1940's and 1950, 1952, 1953, 1955 are the best. White Burgundy should be served like other white wines: cold, with fish or white meat.

Café Brulôt. For 12 servings: prepare in advance, and let stand for several hours, thin strips of lemon and orange peel ($\frac{1}{2}$ fruit each), 3 small cinnamon sticks, 1 tablespoon cloves, 24 cubes of sugar; pour $\frac{3}{4}$ cup brandy over this. When ready to serve, make very strong coffee, preferably with some chicory. Light the brandied mixture in a chafing dish, and ladle the burning liquid. (With lights out, you can pour liquid flame.) Add hot coffee slowly before brandy burns out, stir, and ladle into demi-tasse cups. A more dramatic presentation (and more properly named Brulôt) can be made with special Brulôt equipment: a tray in which alcohol is burned, around a bowl with the brandied mixture, and a long-handled ladle.

Calvados. True Apple Brandy from the Normandy area in France.

Capri. An excellent dry white Italian wine from the Bay of Naples district, but seldom from Capri itself.

Cassis. Black currant liqueur.

Caudle. Spiced hot wine; can also be made with hot ale or tea. It contains beaten egg-yolks and sugar.

Chablis. A distinctive white wine, not sweet, from the area around the town of that name in France.

Champagne. A sparkling white wine from the Rheims district in France. The most festive of wines, and excellent as an appetizer, or with fowl during dinner. Champagnes vary from semi-sweetness to dryness in this order: Doux, Sec, Extra Dry, Brut. Champagne *must* be poured ice-cold, and should *not* be chilled with ice in the glass. To open a bottle: First make sure that it is well chilled. Hold it up at a 45° angle, facing away from you. Untwist and remove the wire, then gently turn (do not pull!) the cork. Turning loosens the cork, and the internal pressure pushes it out — so, while turning the cork,

12

hold it back against the pressure. Properly opened, a champagne bottle puffs — it does not pop and does not overflow. *Champagne Cocktail:* in a champagne glass, wet a lump of sugar with Angostura bitters. Add chilled champagne.

Chartreuse. A pale green (also a yellow) liqueur of aromatic sweetness.

Chateau Bottling. The best wines of the Bordeaux district in France are bottled under the label of the vineyard-owner's house or "chateau." A label reading *Mise en bouteille au chateau* is therefore evidence of a dependable wine — but chateau-bottled wines vary from year to year, while wine-merchants' blends are more uniform. The French government publishes an official list of chateaux classified according to excellence.

Cherry Heering. A cherry-flavored brandy; a sweet after-dinner liqueur.

Chianti. The best-known name in Italian wines. Dry, usually red, and usually from the Tuscany area. Sold in the familiar straw-embellished bottle or *fiasco*.

Cider. Apple juice, which, when it ferments, becomes Hard Cider; when this is distilled, it becomes Apple Brandy.

Claret. The general name for the light red wines of the Bordeaux district and for other wines of that type.

Cobbler. Into a goblet or tall glass, filled with crushed ice, pour: either a spoon or two of sugar syrup, or a sweet fruit cordial; followed by whisky, rum, gin or brandy; the whole worked with a long spoon, and decorated with mint or lemon peel. Drink with a straw.

Cocktail. A mixed drink: hard liquor to which flavoring has been added. A good cocktail is always iced, and almost always tart, and thus an appetizer. The liquor is usually gin, whisky or rum. The flavoring is usually aromatic wine like Vermouth (with gin or whisky); or slightly-sweetened lemon or lime juice (with whisky or rum). In some cocktails egg or cream is used as a flavoring, or mollifier. Usually the less flavoring, the better. Cocktails should be well stirred or well shaken with ice, and strained into 3-ounce stemmed glasses.

Coffee Kirsch. Pour strong after-dinner coffee into demi-tasse cups, ¾ full. For each cup: place a lump of sugar on a spoon, soak with kirsch, and ignite. When the flame is about to die, put the spoon in the coffee.

Cognac. The closely-guarded name of grape brandy from the Cognac district in France; when properly aged, the best in the world. The grape-growers operate under close Government control; each is licensed to distill a named quantity of the raw brandy; and the stills are kept under government lock and key. The raw brandy is bought by the big dealers, who blend and age it; and, when they bottle it, give it a better color with caramel, and reduce it with water to drinkable strength. The longer the brandy is aged in wood the better it is, and the more expensive. The letters commonly found on Cognac labels are supposed to refer to these qualities: V = very; O = old; S = superior; P = pale. Best indication of a fine Cognac: a label stating it has aged 20 years or more.

Cointreau. A colorless aromatic liqueur with orange flavoring.

Collins. A long iced drink. The Tom Collins is the most popular, and uses gin. For each drink: to a tall glass with ice-cubes, add a spoon of sugar syrup, the juice of a lemon, a jigger or more of gin, and soda to fill. Use plenty of ice. Old Tom Gin is sweetened, so if you use it, use less sugar.

Cooler. A decorated highball, like a Horse's Neck. Peel an orange or lemon in a continuous spiral, and hang inside a highball glass. Put in 3-4 ice cubes, 2 ounces or more of liquor, and fill with soda. Sugar syrup may be added to taste.

Cordial. Fruit-flavored wine brandy or grain alcohol.

Cream Sherry. The name given to a specially sweet rich dark Sherry to suggest its blandness.

Crusta. A kind of cocktail Sour served in a specially-prepared glass. Moisten the edge of a small tumbler or large wineglass with lemon; rotate in granulated sugar to get the crusted effect. Garnish inside of glass with a coil of lemon peel and a cherry. The liquor is whisky, brandy, rum or Sherry, with lime or lemon juice added. Shake with ice like a cocktail, and strain into prepared glass. Any cocktail recipe which contains lemon may be used.

Cuban Presidente. 2 ounces white label rum, ½ ounce French Vermouth, 2 dashes Curaçao, 1 dash Grenadine. Stir with ice, garnish with cherry, and twist a piece of lemon peel over the drink.

Curaçao. A pale liqueur from the Dutch West Indies, orange-flavored.

Daiquiri. A Rum Sour. Proportions: 1 part sugar syrup, 2 parts lime juice, 6 parts or more white label rum.

Daiquiri Mint. Add a crushed sprig of mint (or a few drops of white Crème de Menthe) to your shaker, and strain into cocktail glass.

Daiquiri Variations. Add a few drops of Maraschino liqueur, or Curaçao, or Pernod, or Falernum to your shaker. Grenadine instead of sugar makes a pink variety.

Daisy. An iced drink made like any Sour, except that Grenadine or other fruit-flavor sweetening is used instead of sugar. May be strained into a cocktail glass; but better distinguished by being made in a mug or silver goblet filled with crushed ice, worked with a spoon, and served with a short straw. Decorate with fruit and mint.

Drambuie. Scotch liqueur, made from Scotch whisky, heather honey, and various herbs and spices. The only flavoring with which Scotch whisky is really at ease.

Dubonnet. A ruby-colored aromatic wine, called an aperitif by the French, but too sweet for an appetizer to most tastes. Try ice-cold, with a twist of peel.

Eau de Vie. Water of life. A name for brandy made from leavings; *Eau-de-vie de Cidre* is apple brandy from the mash after cider-making; *Eau-de-vie de Marc* is the distillation of fermented grape husks after wine-pressing.

Elderberry Wine. Made from both the flowers and berries: the flowers giving a muscat flavor and the berries giving color.

Falerno. The Falernum of the ancient Romans. Red and white wines are still given that name, but do not justify the praise of the Latin poets.

Falernum. A sweetening liquor of low alcoholic content, almond-flavored; may be substituted for sugar in a rum cocktail.

Fine. (Feen). Name commonly given in France to brandies of unknown or unadmitted sources. Not to be confused with *Fine Champagne*.

Fine Champagne (pronounced Feen). The best of Cognacs; has nothing to do with Champagne, the bubbly wine.

Fix. Like a Daisy, a drink of the Sour type, made with fruit-flavored sweetening in a mug or goblet filled with crushed ice (work the ingredients with a spoon until the mug is frosted), decorated with fruit and mint. Serve with straw. One recipe: 1 part cordial, 2 parts lime, 6 parts Gin.

Fizz. A Sour-type drink, made and shaken like a Whisky Sour or Daiquiri, then strained into an 8-ounce tumbler and "fizzed" with charged water from a siphon bottle. A typical recipe: 1 part sugar syrup, 2 parts lime or lemon juice, 3 parts gin. A *Silver Fizz* has 1 egg-white per drink shaken up with the other ingredients; a *Golden Fizz* has 1 egg yolk per drink.

Flip. Wine or liquor shaken up with sugar and whole egg. Typical recipe: 1 spoon sugar syrup, 1 egg, 2 ounces brandy. Shake with ice, strain into Sour glass. Top with a dash of grated nutmeg.

Frappé. A liquor shaken with — or more commonly, poured into — shaved ice, in a champagne or wine glass, and served with a short straw. Crème de menthe and Pernod are commonly served so. When more than one ingredient is used, shake first with the ice and pour unstrained into the glass. For example the Café Royale frappé: 3 parts black coffee, 1 part brandy.

Frozen Cocktails. Put ingredients, with crushed ice, into an electric blender, and run until foamy. Serve with short straws, heaped in champagne or wine glasses. The commonest frozen cocktail is the Daiquiri.

23

Fruit Brandy. A name commonly given to a Cordial, in which a wine brandy (or even pure alcohol) has been given a sweet fruit flavoring. A true brandy is distilled from the fermented fruit, and retains only a slight fruit flavor.

Geneva. A name given to Dutch gin, also known as Hollands. Genièvre is French for juniper, the flavoring of gin, and presumably the source of the names Geneva and Gin.

Gibson. A Martini with a small cocktail onion instead of an olive. One part vermouth, 6 parts gin. Stir vigorously with ice; strain into stemmed glass.

Gimlet. A short drink like a Rickey: 1 part sugar syrup, 2 parts lime juice, 4 parts gin; add soda water to fill fruit juice or Sour glass. May be served without soda water, as a cocktail. Shake with ice, strain.

Gin. A colorless liquor with flavoring mostly from juniper berries. The basis of the Martini and other cocktails. There are two types: *London:* in which grain alcohol is redistilled with juniper berries

24

and other flavorings. This is the gin used in cocktails. *Geneva, Hollands,* or *Dutch,* in which the juniper berries are added to the grain in the original distillation. This has a much stronger flavor, and is not suitable for cocktails. Old Tom is sweetened London Gin. Yellow gin is — or should be — an aged and superior variety of London Gin. Sloe Gin is not gin but a liqueur.

Ginger Beer. English, slightly alcoholic, effervescent drink, ginger-flavored.

Glogg. A Swedish winter hot drink: Heat in a bowl: 1 quart brandy, ½ cup sugar, 1 dozen cloves, 1-2 sticks cinnamon, ½ cup raisins, ½ cup blanched almonds (not salted). After heating, ignite the brandy, and stir until sugar is dissolved. Add 1 pint warm Sherry or Port. Serve in mugs — preferably warmed beforehand.

Goldwasser. A dry colorless liqueur, citrus-flavored, containing tiny harmless gold-leaf particles which catch the light when the drink is shaken or stirred.

Grand Marnier. A liqueur made with brandy as a base, and orange flavoring.

Grappa. A cheap Italian brandy, distilled not from wine but from the fermented husks of grapes after the juice has been pressed in wine-making.

Graves. One of the wine districts of the Bordeaux area; and white wine from that district in France.

Grenadine. A red sweetening: sugar syrup with coloring.

Grog. Liquor and water; the liquor was normally, on British or other ships where the term was common, Jamaica or other heavy rum. Now usually served hot and sweet, with lemon juice or slice. For each drink: in a mug put a lump of sugar, a slice of lemon, a jigger or more of rum, and hot water to taste. Before pouring hot water, put a spoon in the mug (or glass) to prevent cracking.

Highball. A tall iced drink with liquor and (unless otherwise specified) soda water. The usual highball is Scotch and soda. Rye is usually but not always served with ginger ale, and rum is commonly served with cola.

Hippocras. In the Middle Ages, a wine which had been sweetened and spiced, then filtered through a woolen bag called Hippocrates' sleeve — hence its name.

Hock. A general name for the wines of the German Rheingau district, which produces the finest white wines in the world; and, loosely, for all Rhine wines. The name derives from Hochheim — a district not actually in the Rheingau.

Horse's Neck. Usually this is a non-alcoholic tall glass of ice and ginger ale, with a lemon-peel, cut in a continuous loop, hanging out over the edge of the glass. Liquor may be added before the ginger ale: this is sometimes referred to as Horse's Neck with a Kick.

Hot Buttered Rum. In each mug or glass: 1 lump of sugar, 1 clove or half piece of cinnamon; 1 jigger or more of Jamaica rum; add boiling water and a lump of butter.

Hot Spiced Rum. An excellent recipe: heat sweet apple cider almost to boiling, with 2 sticks of cinnamon. Put 1 ounce or less of rum into each punch or wine glass, add hot cider. If the glass is not thin, a spoon in it prevents cracking.

Irish Coffee. In a pre-heated glass put 1 spoon sugar, fill ¾ full with hot black coffee, add 1½ ounces Irish Whisky, and stir. Top with whipped cream. Since rum and brandy go better with coffee and cream than whisky, non-Irishmen may make a substitution of liquor.

Irish Whisky. Made like Scotch: at least partly from barley malt, but without the smoky taste of Scotch: the smoke from the peat-fires traditionally used to dry the malt is not, as in Scotland, allowed to filter through the grain.

Jamaica Rum. Heavy dark flavorful distillate from molasses and sugar cane, which has been allowed to ferment naturally before distillation. Jamaica cannot be substituted for Cuban rum in cocktails, but is superior to it for long fruit drinks like the Planter's Punch.

Jersey Lightning. Slang name for raw Applejack.

Julep. Tall iced drink, from the Persian *julap:* sweet drink. Prepare chilled glasses with crushed ice. For each drink mix 1 tablespoon sugar syrup, 1-2 dashes bitters, a dozen mint leaves (young, fresh, washed, slightly bruised), and 2 ounces bourbon. Pour into crushed ice in glasses, from which any melted ice has first been poured off. Stir up and down with long spoon, add ice, and bourbon to taste. Holding with clean napkin, stir again until glass frosts. Insert straw. Garnish with mint sprig, washed and sugared.

Kava. (Also *Ava, Arva, Yava*). A Polynesian fermentation of the sweet mash obtained from roots of a type of pepper plant.

Kirsch. A colorless brandy made from fermented cherry juice; not a cherry cordial. Also called Kirschwasser.

Kumiss (also *Koumiss*). Fermented milk; in the Asian uplands, mares' and asses' milk is used.

Kummel. A colorless liqueur with flavoring that noticeably includes caraway.

Kvass. A Russian home-made beverage: the fermentation of a mash of malt, rye, sugar and water.

Lachryma Christi. A white still wine made on the slopes of Mt. Vesuvius; also a sparkling variety. Its name (Tears of Christ) has given it a special fame.

Liqueur. A general term for the sweet, powerful, flavored drinks made by infusing or redistilling various herb and other flavorings with (usually) grape brandy. Famous liqueurs include Benedictine, Chartreuse, Cointreau, Curaçao, Grand Marnier, Drambuie, Strega. Serve in very small quantities in a tiny glass after dinner; or use, in minute quantities, as a flavoring for cocktails.

London Gin. As opposed to Dutch or Hollands Gin, this is the type used for Martinis and other cocktails. The name does *not* mean the gin is made in England: witness the label of a famous brand:

DISTILLED LONDON DRY GIN

DISTILLED	& BOTTLED
IN LINDEN	NEW JERSEY

Madeira. A fortified aperitif wine from Madeira, similar to Sherry, and — like Sherry — produced in varying degrees of sweetness. A common drink in Colonial days in America.

Maguey. A Mexican distillation of fermented Agave (aloe) sap.

Malaga. A sweet Spanish dessert wine.

Malmsey. A sweet dessert wine from Cyprus, Madeira and the Canary Islands.

Manhattan. After the Martini, the most popular of all cocktails. One part sweet Vermouth, 3 parts rye or bourbon whisky, a dash or two of bitters. Stir with ice, strain, and serve with cherry.

Maraschino. A liqueur made from Marasca cherries, as well as the cherries in syrup.

Marc. A cheap French brandy, distilled not from wine but from the fermented husks of the grapes after the juice has been pressed in wine making. Also called Eau de Vie.

Margaux. One of the great wine-producing districts of the Bordeaux area.

Marsala. A fortified sweet dessert wine from Sicily.

Martini. The most famous and popular cocktail — and the most argued about. The present trend is toward a Martini extremely dry — that is, almost all gin. This trend has gone so far that it is sure to reverse itself. With the best gin, use the following recipe: 1 part dry Vermouth, 5-6 parts gin, stir with ice, strain, and serve with small olive if desired, or twist lemon peel over drink, and drop in. With poorer gin, use a smaller proportion. The Martini can be made with vodka — like gin a low-flavored liquor; some drinkers claim less let-down after Vodka Martinis.

Mead. An ancient liquor made from fermented malt, honey, and water, usually with spice or other flavoring added.

Médoc. A great Bordeaux wine district.

Mirabelle. A colorless liqueur distilled from the Mirabelle plum.

Mojito. A West Indian tall drink: Squeeze ½ lime into a highball glass, add a spoon of sugar syrup, some mint leaves, and fill glass with shaved ice. Pour 2 ounces white label rum into glass, stir well with bar spoon (or swizzle), add a little soda water to fill, and stir again.

Moselle. A light white wine similar to the Rhine wines.

Mulled Wine. Wine heated and flavored with nutmeg and other spices. Traditional way to heat the wine: a red-hot poker.

Muscatel. A name given to some sweet fortified dessert wines; sometimes with flavoring from elderberry flowers.

Myrtle Bank. A West Indies punch. Fill a highball glass with cracked ice. Into it pour — first shaking with ice — 2 ounces 151-proof Demerara rum, juice of ½ lime, 6 dashes Grenadine, 1 teaspoon sugar syrup. On top of the glass float a spoon of Maraschino liqueur.

Napoleon Brandy. One device of Cognac bottlers to suggest great age is to put

the name of Napoleon, and a picture of him, on the label. Presumably the bottler does this to his best or oldest varieties. Brandy ages only in the cask; so cobwebs, "time-stained" labels, or other marks of age on the bottle mean nothing.

Natur, also *Naturwein.* Unsugared and unblended wine — and thus presumably superior.

Negus. Wine spiced, sweetened, heated, and diluted by hot water.

Okolehao, or *Oke.* A Hawaiian distillation of fermented mash of cane-sugar, rice lees and the juice of baked Taro root. It has the strength of whisky, is colored dark brown, and has a smoky flavor.

Old-Fashioned. Considered one of the standard cocktails; but actually Whisky on the Rocks with a little sugar and bitters. Into an Old-fashioned glass or stubby tumbler put a spoon of sugar syrup, 2-3 dashes bitters, a jigger of rye or bourbon, and stir. Add two cubes of ice (preferably cracked) and more whisky if desired. Garnish with a lemon peel — first twisting it over drink — and a cherry. For frivolous drinkers, use also a pineapple stick and half an orange slice.

Old Tom Gin. A sweetened London Gin which gave its name to the Tom Collins. If used in the Collins or other gin drinks requiring sugar, omit sugar, or at least add sugar to taste.

On the Rocks. A popular way to take whisky: a jigger of liquor poured over a cube or two of ice in an Old-fashioned glass. Mixed drinks like the Martini and Manhattan are sometimes prepared in the same way as a short-cut for a single serving.

Orgeat. A sweet non-alcoholic flavoring made of sugar syrup and ground almonds. Excellent instead of sugar in rum drinks.

Orvieto. One of the best Italian wines. White, often slightly sweet.

Ouzo. A Greek cordial, anis-flavored, served with water before meals.

Pajarete. Spanish sweet dessert wine.

Parfait Amour. similar to Crème de Violette and Crème Yvette — a violet-flavored liqueur.

Pernod. The manufacturer of, and the trade name for, a non-poisonous Absinthe manufactured since the real thing was outlawed many years ago. Licorice- or anise-flavored green liquor, usually taken with ice and water or in a frappé. Herb-saint is an American equivalent.

Perry. Fermented juice of pears — as hard cider is of apples.

Peychaud. A variety of bitters recommended to be used in the Sazerac cocktail.

Pilsner Beer. Lager beer from Pilsen; and domestic lagers in imitation.

Piquillin. A South American fruit from which a sort of brandy is made by distilling its fermented juice.

Pisco. A fiery distillation from Peru.

Planter's Punch. A tall Summer drink with Jamaica rum, various fruit juices, and soda. Often made on the 1, 2, 3, 4 formula: 1 part sugar syrup, 2 parts lemon juice, 3 parts Jamaica rum, 4 parts water, soda, or tea. Pour all but the soda into a tall glass packed with crushed ice. Fill with soda to near top, and work with long spoon. Variations: fruit syrup instead of sugar; orange juice in addition to lemon juice. Try also fresh tea instead of soda.

Pony. One ounce. A pony of brandy in a small brandy glass is enough; somewhat more should be served in a large snifter.

Port Wine. A sweet fortified wine from Portugal. In making Port, brandy is added to the fermenting wine-grape vat. This extra alcohol brings the brew to a stable alcoholic content before all the grape sugar turns to alcohol. The wine is therefore sweeter and stronger than wines in which the fermentation is allowed to complete itself naturally. The best of each year is set aside as "Vintage" Port. The balance is blended with older stocks to maintain a constant quality. *Tawny Port* is aged in wood, is light in body, and is less alcoholic than *Ruby Port*, a blend of Tawny and new wines.

40

Posset. Sweetened and spiced milk or cream which has been curdled by adding hot ale or wine. Eggs (whites and yolks separately beaten) may be added to the milk, or substituted for it. Mix well, serve in cups or mugs, with grated nutmeg.

Pousse-Café. A colorful creation in a special straight-sided liqueur glass, and containing differently-colored liqueurs and cordials in horizontal layers. The liqueurs must be poured in order of heaviness: usually the more sugar content the heavier. They are poured slowly down the inner side of the glass from a spoon or small glass; or poured over the back of a spoon held inside the glass and inserted into the previous layer. Often topped with a spoon of cream. Making and handling this drink takes skill.

Prairie Oyster. A supposed cure for a hangover: Mix in a tumbler or Old-fashioned glass 1 ounce brandy, 1 tablespoon vinegar, 1 tablespoon Worcestershire, 1 teaspoon ketchup, 1 teaspoon bitters. Gently add the unbroken yolk of an egg, and swallow whole without retching — if you can.

Pulque. The fermented sap of the Maguey plant, from Mexico. When this fermented juice is distilled, it produces a variety of brandy called Tequila.

Punch. A mixture of liquors, fruit juices, fruit and carbonated beverages which, because it can be made in large quantities in a bowl, is a popular party drink. But it can also be made in a smaller quantity in a pitcher — in which case it is called a Cup; or even in individual glasses, as in the Planter's Punch. In addition to the usual punches which use citrus fruits and juices, there are Milk Punches which can be served either cold or hot.

It is easy to make a good punch from assorted common liquids, if a few basic rules are followed: Use not more than 25% liquor — and use *much* less for young people or people who seldom drink. Use not more than 25% fruit juices — of which only a small part should be lemon or lime. Use 50% or more carbonated beverages; a part of this can be cold tea or cider.

For the basic liquor: Don't use Scotch whisky. If you use gin, don't use any other hard liquor. You can combine American whiskies, rum, and brandy. White wine will combine with any of the liquors; red wine will make a red punch. Champagne adds glamor to a punch *only* if it is added with a flourish just before serving. Otherwise ginger ale will do as well. Pour all ingredients except carbonated waters over a large block of ice or a mound of ice cubes, and let stand up to an hour; then add carbonated waters and serve. In figuring quantities, allow 3-4 ounces per drink — probably at least 3 drinks per person — but remember that some of the ice will melt and add to your total quantity.

Quetsch. A colorless brandy made from plums.

Quinquina. An aromatic wine with quinine as a flavoring element.

Ramos Gin Fizz. A New Orleans drink: 2 ounces gin, 1½ ounces cream, juice of ½ lemon and ½ lime, 1 teaspoon sugar syrup, 1 white of egg, 2 drops vanilla extract, 3-4 drops orange flower water (if available), 1 squirt soda. Shake, shake and shake with plenty of ice, and strain into tall thin glass. There are several variants, each being "guaranteed original."

Ratafia. Old-fashioned fruit cordial, high in alcohol, often homemade.

Retsina. The name used for the resinated wines of Greece.

Rhine. The great German wine district is along the slopes bordering the Rhine River. The Rheingau is the best section of this district. In general Rhine wines are pale, light, low in alcoholic content, and a trifle sweet.

Rhone. The vineyards along the Rhone River in southern France generally produce red and white wines less famous than the Bordeaux and Burgundy districts; but Tavel, a pink wine, is the best rosé in France. Hermitage and Chateauneuf de Pape are good red wines.

Rickey. A Summer drink. One teaspoon sugar syrup, 1 oz. lime juice, 2 oz. liquor. Pour over 2-3 ice cubes in a medium-size glass, and fill with soda. The Gin Rickey is a favorite, but other liquors may be used. So may apricot or other sweet fruit cordials — in which case omit the sugar. This makes a pleasant variant.

Rob Roy. Manhattan made with Scotch.

Rose. A modified Martini cocktail, with raspberry syrup or Grenadine to make it pink; decorated with a cherry. Add 1 spoon of the coloring per drink to shaker. A variant: 3 parts Kirsch, 1 part dry vermouth, 1 spoon per drink of the coloring.

Rosé. A pink wine: Tavel is the best.

Rum. A liquor made from sugar-cane molasses, chiefly in the Caribbean. There are three varieties: White Label: clear, pale, lightly flavored; Gold Label: darker and with more flavor; Tropical (usually Jamaica), dark, heavy, pungent, in which the molasses flavor has not been filtered out. In cocktails the White Label is usually best. In tall drinks like the Planters' Punch, where there is a lot of fruit and soda to dilute the flavor, the Jamaica is best, as it is for rum flavoring in cooking.

Rye Whisky. A distillation of grain mash, at least 51% rye, but including barley and corn. In general, the older the whisky (the longer it has been aged in casks) the better. Usually blended — with grain alcohol or new whisky; but you get more *whisky* for your money if you buy a bonded brand: all aged whisky.

St. Emilion. One of the great wine districts of the Bordeaux area.

Sack. A name formerly common for a dry Sherry (from *sec* or *secco*).

Sake. A kind of Japanese beer made from a double fermentation of rice, but stronger than beer. Served warm in tiny porcelain bowls.

Sangaree. A sweetened beer, wine or liquor, served in a tall glass and dusted with grated nutmeg. For beer and ale: 2 spoons of sugar syrup in an 8-ounce glass, fill with cold beer, stir, and dust with nutmeg. For wine: use a couple of ice cubes in the glass. For fortified wines like Port and Sherry: less sugar, and use half wine and half ice-water.

Sangria. Spanish wine cup. In a pitcher with ice, drop slices of orange, add sugar syrup to taste, and approximately equal parts red wine and carbonated water.

Saumur. French sparkling wine of the Champagne type.

Sauternes. A sweet white wine from the Bordeaux region of France. Should be chilled in the refrigerator before serving; it is best with fowl or dessert. Properly spelled with the final "s".

Sazerac. A New Orleans cocktail, really a modified Old-fashioned: 2 ounces rye or bourbon, 1 teaspoon sugar syrup, 2-3 dashes Peychaud bitters, 2 dashes Pernod. Stir with ice, and pour into Old-fashioned glass with 2 or more ice-cubes.

Schnapps. Properly, Geneva or Hollands gin, but also applied to whisky and other hard liquors.

Scotch Whisky. A distillation from barley and (traditionally) barley malt, and deriving its smoky flavor from the peat fires over which the malt is dried.

Shandy Gaff. Half ale and half ginger ale. Pour separately into glass or mug and stir, or pour simultaneously. The bottles should be cold.

Sherry. A fortified aperitif wine from Spain which derives its name from the town of Jerez. To the new wine of the Jerez district, as it ferments, grape brandy is added; this brings the brew to a stable alcoholic content while there is still grape sugar not converted to alcohol: making it stronger and sweeter than table wines. The usual kinds of Sherry: *Fino*, pale and dry, to be served cold as an appetizer; *Amontillado*, less pale and dry but also served cold as an appetizer; *Oloroso* and *Amoroso*, medium-sweet and medium dark, served at room temperature but not as appetizers; *Golden*, *Brown*, or *Solera*, heavy, sweet, and dark, served at room temperature. So-called Cream Sherry is sweet and heavy. Dry Sherry may be substituted for Vermouth in Martinis.

Shrub. An aged mixture of fruit juices, sugar, and hard liquor — usually brandy or Jamaica Rum. A homemade cordial.

Sling. For all practical purposes, another name for Toddy; like the toddy it can be served hot or cold. Two ounces rum or other hard liquor, lemon juice or a slice of lemon, a spoon of sugar or syrup, with cold water or soda water in Summer; and boiling water in Winter. (Keep a spoon in the glass to forestall cracking.)

Slivovitz. A pale-colored prune or plum brandy, usually but not necessarily raw.

Sloe Gin. A liqueur — not a true gin — made from sloeberries.

Smash. A drink made with mint leaves —and thus a kind of julep. For each drink, bruise a sprig of mint, add a spoon of sugar syrup (and bitters if desired), 2 ounces liquor, and shake with ice. If served in a cocktail glass, decorate with mint leaf and cherry; in a Sour glass fruit may be added, for the quantity of liquor is small. This defect can also be overcome by serving the drink poured over crushed ice, as a frappé.

Sour. One of the basic types of cocktail: 1 part sugar syrup, 2 parts lemon or lime juice, 6 or more parts liquor. Thus the Whisky Sour, Rum Sour (Daiquiri), Brandy Sour, Gin Sour. Many variations possible: sweet fruit juices, or very small amounts of cordials, instead of sugar.

50

Southern Comfort. A liqueur with a bourbon base, peach-flavored. Can be substituted in cocktails where whisky is specified; but it will make sweet drinks unless there is sugar in the recipe which can be omitted, as in the Old-fashioned, Whisky Sour, Julep, etc. In a Southern Comfort Manhattan, try dry Vermouth instead of sweet.

Sparkling Wines. Wines in which the fermentation is completed in the corked bottle, so that gas produced by fermentation remains in solution until the cork is removed. Some poorer sparkling wines are made by forcing gas into still wines before bottling. Champagne is the great sparkling wine.

Spatlese. German name for the wines made from late-picked (ripest and sweetest) grapes.

Spritzer. A wine highball, approximately half wine and half soda. But properly made only with Rhine or other light German wines, with carbonated water from a seltzer bottle, and using cold ingredients but no ice.

Stirrup Cup. A punch, normally served in a tall glass with ice, and decorated with lemon peel. One recipe: 1 teaspoon brown sugar (dissolved in same quantity of water), juice of ½ lime, 1 ounce pineapple juice, 2 ounces rum, soda to fill.

Stout. The darkest and sweetest type of beer or ale. Porter is weak, sweet, Stout.

Strega. A sweet, golden Italian liqueur.

Swedish Punch. Common name for Arrack Punsch, a sweet liqueur.

Swizzle. A drink made by twirling a swizzle stick (between the palms) in the ingredients to mix and aerate them. Usually the drink is a Sour, with Jamaica rum. The Swizzle can be made individually in a tumbler or Old-fashioned glass with shaved ice; or in a pitcher (until it frosts if it is silver) and poured into cocktail glasses. The swizzle stick has protruding blades at the foot to churn the liquid. One conservative definition of the Swizzle: Jamaica rum and soft water — soft water being necessary for the foamy effect.

Syllabub. A sweet heavy drink made from equal parts of sweet Sherry (or other fortified wines), milk and cream, and with sugar to taste. Beat together and pour into champagne glasses. Really a dessert in itself; but formally as a dessert, soak a piece of cake in the wine, place in a saucer champagne glass, and pour Syllabub over it. Rum or brandy can be added to the ingredients; and sometimes a little lemon juice is substituted for the milk.

Tafia. A West Indian name for rum distilled from molasses, as opposed to the original form of rum, distilled from fermented sugar-cane juice.

Tequilla. A kind of brandy, a distillation from fermented Maguey pulp called Pulque, from Mexico.

Toddy. A sweetened drink of liquor and water, with a slice of lemon and sprinkled with cinnamon. Usually served hot: in a mug place 1 spoon sugar syrup, slice of lemon or piece of lemon peel, and 2 ounces rum or other liquor. Add boiling water. Keep a spoon in the glass to prevent cracking. Also may be served cold, but why?

Toddy. In tropical areas, the sap of palm-trees, and beverages fermented from it.

Tokay. Hungarian dessert wines from the Tokaj district; *not* made from the so-called Tokay grape. Next to the rare *Essence, Aszu* is the sweetest — over-ripe grapes are added to the making.

Tom and Jerry. A hot toddy combined with egg-nog. For each person beat 1 egg, white and yolk separately; with a teaspoon of sugar and a teaspoon or more of cinnamon and/or other spices mixed in with the yolk. Add also a tablespoon of Jamaica rum. Fold in whites. Put mixture in large mug, add a jigger or more of bourbon, and fill with hot milk or water. Stir till the whole drink foams. Dust with nutmeg.

Tom Collins. A standard Summer tall drink. For each drink: juice of 1 lemon (1 ounce), a tablespoon or more of sugar syrup, and 2 or more ounces of gin. Pour into tall glass, with 3-4 ice-cubes, fill with soda, stir, and serve with a sprig of mint, a slice of lime or lemon, or a cherry. Old Tom Gin, which is sweetened, may be used, in which case add sugar to taste.

Triple Sec. A citrus-flavored colorless liqueur like Cointreau.

Vermouth. An aromatic wine made by treating white wine with infusions of aromatic herbs. It can be drunk straight (it is best with ice and a twist of lemon, with or without soda) or mixed in cocktails and other drinks. *Italian Vermouth* is sweet; it can be used as an afternoon drink, but is too sweet to make a good before-dinner appetizer. It is used in the Manhattan. *French Vermouth* is dry, and may be used as an appetizer. It is used in the Martini. Many contemporary dry Vermouths are very much paler in color and flavor than they used to be, to satisfy the present demand for pale, almost flavorless, Martinis. Such Vermouths, with lemon-peel, make excellent appetizers.

Vermouth Cassis. A Summer drink served in a medium-size highball glass. One ounce Crème de Cassis, 1½ ounces or more dry French Vermouth, 2 ice-cubes. Stir, add soda, stir again, and serve. Other aperitif wines like Dubonnet, St. Raphael, and Byrrh may be substituted for the Cassis.

Vieille Cure. An aromatic liqueur made by a religious order in France. The name means Old Vicarage and does not carry an accent.

Usquebaugh. The original Celtic name for the ancestor of our whisky.

Vintage Years. In the case of most French, German and Italian wines the year of the vintage is important as an index to quality — though a good year on the bottle is no guarantee that the wine inside is good. Many French and Italian wines do not carry a vintage date — which means that they are blends, but does not mean they are inferior. Burgundy often does not carry a date. California vintages are more consistent than European, and their dates are less significant. The best recent dates on European wines are 1947, 1949, 1950, 1952, 1953, 1955.

Vodka. A kind of colorless grain whisky, originally from Poland and Russia. It is commonly believed that Vodka is a potato whisky: but while its alcohol could come from the distillation of a potato mash, it actually comes traditionally from wheat and rye, which are more plentiful than potatoes in Russia. Since Vodka has only the slightest kind of flavor, it is a good mixing agent, and is currently popular in the Martini (where it is said to minimize the letdown after the lift) Bloody Mary, Screwdriver, and Vodka and Tonic.

Bloody Mary: 3 ounces tomato juice, 1 oz. lemon juice, 1½ oz. vodka, Worcestershire, salt, pepper. Shake with ice; strain.

Screwdriver: 1½ ounces vodka in a tall glass with ice. Fill with orange juice.

Vouvray. Town on the Loire River, source of white wines of that name.

Wassail Bowl. An English traditional drink. For 18 servings: Heat 1 quart ale almost to boiling point; into it stir grated nutmeg, powdered ginger, and grated peel of 1 lemon. While ale is heating, beat up 3 eggs with 4 ounces moistened white sugar. Use 2 heated pitchers: into one put hot ale and beaten eggs. Into the other put 1 quart warmed rum or brandy. Pour mixture from one bowl to the other until it is smooth, then pour into holly-wreathed pre-heated bowl. Other recipes vary widely: using hot Sherry, for example, instead of a combination of ale and hard liquor.

Whisky. An alcoholic liquor made by the distillation of grain. Scotch is made traditionally from barley malt (barley which has been moistened, allowed to sprout, and then kiln-dried) but is no longer 100% malt. Rye is made from at least 51% rye, bourbon from corn; but some barley malt is used in the making of all good whiskies.

Wine Cooler. Peel an orange or lemon in a continuous spiral, and hang inside a highball glass. Put in 3 or 4 ice cubes, 3-4 ounces wine, and fill with soda. With a dry wine, a little sugar may be added. With a sweet wine, a little lemon juice.

Zubrowka. Russian vodka in which Zubrowka grass has been steeped to give color, flavor and bouquet.

Zombie. A king-size drink which always impresses the recipient. For each drink use: 1 teaspoon Falernum or other sweetening, 1/2 ounce lime juice, 1 ounce pineapple juice, 2 teaspoons apricot cordial, 3 ounces white and/or gold label rum, 1 ounce Jamaica rum. Shake all ingredients with crushed ice, and pour, with ice, into a very tall glass (16 ounces). Decorate with lemon and orange peel, colored cherries, mint, pineapple. Dust with powdered sugar. A spoon of high-proof rum or brandy may be floated on top of the drink before decorating.

IMPORTANT POSTSCRIPT

Hair of the Dog. Some sufferers from hangover think that they can relieve it by taking more of what caused their trouble in the first place. This they call: taking a hair of the dog that bit you. A better relief for the acidity caused by alcohol is an antacid: either a drugstore remedy or milk. Hot coffee will make you feel better.

Hangover. The best way to avoid a hangover is to be moderate. The next best way is to drink some olive oil beforehand; this will discourage the alcohol from being absorbed into the stomach lining and so into the blood-stream. And space out your drinks!

THIS VOLUME IS DESIGNED, PRINTED
AND PUBLISHED AT THE OFFICE OF
THE PETER PAUPER PRESS
MOUNT VERNON
NEW YORK